Muffles' Measurement Models
Part Two: The Metric System

Catherine Twomey Fosnot
Catherine Henchey

New Perspectives on Learning, LLC
1194 Ocean Avenue
New London, CT 06320

Copyright © 2017 Catherine Twomey Fosnot and Catherine Henchey
All rights reserved.
ISBN: 0-9976886-4-5
ISBN-13: 978-0-9976886-4-1

Table of Contents

Unit Overview 2

Day 1 – Patricio's Line 11
Students are reintroduced to Muffles and work to find the length of a line using metric units.

Day 2 – How Long is the Line? 16
Students discuss converting metric measurements of length during a minilesson, gallery walk, and math congress.

Day 3 – Patricio's Model 21
A minilesson and Patricio's model of a new problem provide students opportunities to develop multiplicative structuring and work with the ratio table model.

Day 4 – How Long a Wait? 27
Students discuss converting measurements of length and time during a minilesson, gallery walk, and math congress.

Day 5 – Muffles' Recipes 30
Students make recipe charts for Muffles using proportional scaling with new units of measurement for volume and weight.

Day 6 – Muffles' Dark Chocolate Truffles 35
Students discuss their work from Day Five and have another opportunity to scale using place value patterns in a minilesson after the math congress.

Day 7 – Chocolate Nut Truffles 40
Students deepen their understanding of proportional relationships as they puzzle over Muffles' intentions for a new recipe chart.

Day 8 – The Chart for the Truffles 47
Students begin the day with another minilesson using the ratio table model and then discuss their insights from Day Seven.

Day 9 – Prices by the Pound 50
Students scale weight and money together after Muffles decides to sell his famous truffles by the ounce.

Day 10 – Choose Your Own Numbers 53
Students make use of all of the strategies for conversion and ratio tables they have developed during the unit as they create their own numbers for Muffles' price chart.

Appendices 56

Unit Overview

This unit is the second of two related, companion units for grade 4 focused on the development of measurement. The first unit focuses on the Customary U.S. units; this unit focuses on place value and the metric system. Muffles, a baker, is introduced to students in *Muffles' Truffles*, a previous CFLM unit that provides various opportunities to explore multiplication using arrays.

Muffles returns in *Muffles' Measurement Models (Parts One and Two).* He expands his business and several problems related to measurement arise. For one, he needs conversion tables for his recipes! Children explore measurement conversions and develop several tables for converting liters to milliliters, pounds to ounces, inches to feet and yards, centimeters to meters and kilometers, grams to kilograms, minutes to hours and seconds, and dollars to dimes and pennies. Children are asked to select and use an appropriate measurement unit, to compare and relate the measurements, to construct the need for decomposition of units into smaller units, and to use operations to convert units. The models used throughout are the double number line for equivalence and the ratio table for scaling and proportional reasoning. The units are designed to align with the CCSS Standards of Mathematical Practice and the following core objectives:

Measurement & Data 4.MD: Solve problems involving measurement and conversion of measurements.

CCSS.Math.Content.4.MD.A.1

Know relative sizes of measurement units within one system of units including km, m, cm; kg, g; lb, oz.; l, ml; hr, min, sec. Within a single system of measurement, express measurements in a larger unit in terms of a smaller unit. Record measurement equivalents in a two-column table. *For example, know that 1 ft is 12 times as long as 1 in. Express the length of a 4 ft snake as 48 in. Generate a conversion table for feet and inches listing the number pairs (1, 12), (2, 24), (3, 36), ...*

CCSS.Math.Content.4.MD.A.2

Use the four operations to solve word problems involving distances, intervals of time, liquid volumes, masses of objects, and money, including problems involving simple fractions or decimals, and problems that require expressing measurements given in a larger unit in terms of a smaller unit. Represent measurement quantities using diagrams such as number line diagrams that feature a measurement scale.

The Landscape of Learning

BIG IDEAS
❖ Smaller units produce a greater value than larger units
❖ Larger units can encompass (and be decomposed into) smaller units
❖ Unitizing
❖ Equivalent measurements can be exchanged
❖ Place value patterns occur when multiplying or dividing by the base
❖ Proportional reasoning
STRATEGIES
❖ Uses standard units and counts
❖ Chooses appropriate unit in relation to object being measured
❖ Decomposes and switches units when needed
❖ Converts using skip counting
❖ Converts using partial products
❖ Scales by doubling
❖ Scales by halving
❖ Scales using place value patterns
❖ Generalized scaling using the operations of multiplication and division
MODELS
❖ Double Number Line
❖ Ratio Table

The Mathematical Landscape

By fourth grade most children have become fairly competent in measuring. For example, when measuring length they iterate a single unit (such as a ruler or meter stick). They place the units back-to-back without gaps and they know the size of the unit matters—smaller units produce a greater value than larger units, yet the measurements are equivalent. They may even know that time is measured in minutes and hours and weight is measured in grams, kilograms, and/or pounds and ounces. However, they usually have little understanding of the exact relationships of the units, for example the exact relationship of inches to feet and feet to yards, or centimeters to the meter stick, or liters to milliliters, etc. They also do not yet have efficient strategies for converting from one unit to another.

The investigations in these two companion units involve children in choosing appropriate tools for more exact measurement and converting from one unit to another. *Muffles' Measurement Models, Part One* focuses on the Customary U.S. measurement tools and conversion within that system. *Muffles' Measurement Models, Part Two* focuses on place value and the metric system. Both units provide children with partially filled out measurement tables. To become able to convert easily from one measure to another, students need a complex network of relations comprised of some big ideas, strategies, and models as shown on the Landscape of Learning on page 10. A description of each follows.

BIG IDEAS

As children explore the investigations within the two units, several big ideas arise. These include:

- ***Smaller units produce a greater value than larger units***
- ***Larger units can encompass (and be decomposed into) smaller units***
- ***Unitizing***
- ***Equivalent measurements can be exchanged***
- ***Place value patterns occur when multiplying or dividing by the base***
- ***Proportional reasoning***

❖ *Smaller units produce a greater value than larger units*

Within a single measurable attribute (mass, volume, time, length, etc.) there are both large and small standardized units. As children measure with these standard units, they construct the idea that when larger units are used the overall measurement will be a smaller number and reciprocally, when smaller units are used the overall measurement will be a greater number.

❖ *Larger units can encompass (and be decomposed into) smaller units*

Iterated smaller units (like inches) can be grouped into larger units (like feet), which in turn can be grouped into yards. As children come to realize that if larger units are used, less would be needed, they can more appropriately choose a unit to use to measure a given object. A 10 ft line might better be measured with a foot-long ruler than with inches, whereas a line less than a foot long might be best to measure in inches. On the other hand, a larger unit may need to be decomposed for exactness. For example, measuring a 10 ft line with a yardstick would require decomposing the last yard into feet.

❖ *Unitizing*

With number, unitizing a group of 10 objects into 1 ten is a big idea. It requires multiplicative thinking as children grapple to understand 132, not just as 100 + 30 + 2, but as 13 tens, plus 2, and later as 13.2 tens. The case is no different with measurement units. As children compose and decompose units, they come to understand that a kilometer can simultaneously be seen as 1,000 meters, or as 100,000 centimeters. A yard can be seen as 3 feet, or as 36 inches.

❖ **Equivalent measurements can be exchanged**

Once children construct conservation of length and unitizing and have had ample opportunities to work with a variety of measurement units, they begin to understand that various units can be used to describe length and distance (or mass, volume, and time), and that equivalent pieces can be exchanged. For example, time can be measured in hours or in minutes: 1½ hours = 90 minutes. One pint plus one cup is equivalent to 1½ pints. Both measurements are correct and may be interchanged to compare or more exactly describe the amount.

❖ Place value patterns occur when multiplying or dividing by the base

Our decimal, or "base-10" number system, is built on tens—each successive place value to the left is generated by multiplying by ten (or dividing, as you move right). The metric system is similarly based on 10 and, along with money, affords ample opportunities for children to multiply and divide by the base. Precisely because multiplication is commutative, an interesting thing happens when students multiply by the base: the factor "moves over" to the appropriate column. For example, 10 x 4 = 4 + 4 + 4 + 4 + 4 + 4 + 4 + 4 + 4 + 4 = 40. The result of 40 seems amazing to students, who often say that they "added a zero," or refer to the pattern as the zero trick. The reason this works is that the 10 groups of 4 can also be thought of as 4 groups of 10—so the 4 is placed into the tens column to show that value and the unitizing of 40 into 4 groups of 10. It is important to support students in exploring why place value patterns occur—to help them construct how place value and the commutative property are involved. As students explore the metric system these ideas are extended further, as now they are multiplying and dividing by 100 and 1,000 as well.

❖ Proportional reasoning

As children work to convert one unit into another, they are developing proportional reasoning. They are dealing with ratios. The logic is: if 100 centimeters equal 1 meter, then 500 centimeters equal 5 meters. Scaling both units up proportionally keeps the conversion rate constant.

STRATEGIES

As you work with the activities in this unit, you will notice that students will use many strategies to solve the problems that are posed to them. Here are some strategies to notice:

- ❖ *Uses standard units and counts*
- ❖ *Chooses an appropriate unit in relation to object being measured*
- ❖ *Decomposes and switches units when needed*
- ❖ *Converts using skip counting*
- ❖ *Converts using partial products*
- ❖ *Scales by doubling*
- ❖ *Scales by halving*
- ❖ *Scales using place value patterns*
- ❖ *Generalized scaling using the operations of multiplication and division*

❖ Uses standard units and counts

Once children construct the idea that a standard unit is necessary for reliable measurement comparisons, they carefully mark the endpoints and count. When asked to convert to a different size unit within the same system, they do not convert, however. They just switch tools, measure again, and count.

❖ Chooses appropriate unit in relation to object being measured

Once children are comfortable understanding a variety of tools they begin to become aware that certain tools have limitations and assets. They no longer just choose a tool and estimate the leftover. They know different tools allow for exactness when needed and they choose an appropriate tool to work with depending on the task.

❖ Decomposes and switches units when needed

Once children construct the big idea that equivalent measurements can be exchanged, a multitude of possible conversions results. Something that measures 48 inches is equivalent in length to something that measures 4 feet. But also, something that measures 1 ft 6 inches can be thought of as 1.5 feet, as 18 inches, or as ½ of a yard. With the metric system, something that measures a meter plus 50 cm can be thought of as 1.5 meters, 150 cm, 15 decimeters, or as 1 ½ meters. Some children may even become intrigued with the relationship between a centimeter and an inch. The conversion rate of 2.54 centimeters = 1 inch is quite close to 2 ½ cm for every inch, and you may find some of your children saying 5 cm is the same as 2 inches, so 10 cm must be 4 inches, etc. Although this is not an exact conversion, encourage it, as it is a great estimate and an early form of proportional reasoning! A pound is equal to 0.45 kilograms, so 2 pounds equal 0.90 kilos, and 4 pounds are 1.8 kilos. Encourage this scaling even though it will not formally be a focus until grade 5.

❖ Converts using skip counting

Skip counting is an advance from counting. Rather than exchanging tools and measuring again, children skip count. For example, to convert 30 yards into feet, children skip count by threes; to convert meters into centimeters, they skip count by hundreds.

❖ Converts using partial products

Using partial products is an advance over skip counting. Knowing that the conversion of 15 yards into feet requires 15 x 3, students might use (10 x 3) + (5 x 3).

❖ Scales by doubling

Doubling is the place most children start when they begin to use proportional reasoning. It is the bridge between additive and multiplicative structuring. If 1 foot is equal to 12 inches, then 2 feet must equal 24 inches. It is a bridge to more generalized scaling because the doubling can still be seen as 12 + 12.

❖ Scales by halving

Halving is similar in terms of being a bridge, but doubling is usually easier in the same way that multiplication is easier for children than division.

❖ Scales using place value patterns

Once students construct the big idea that place value patterns occur when multiplying or dividing by the base, they recognize that the metric system presents many opportunities to take advantage of the place value structure. As students develop their proportional reasoning within the metric system, they will soon begin multiplying and dividing by 10, 100, and 1,000 to scale and convert between units.

❖ Generalized scaling using the operations of multiplication and division

Scaling is an advance over partial products, doubling, and halving as now multiplicative structuring is truly at play. Once the critical precursors (place value patterns, unitizing, proportional reasoning and multiplicative structuring) have been constructed, generalized scaling becomes automatic. In the metric system, if 1 kilogram is 1000 grams, then 4 kilograms equals 4000 grams and 8 kilograms equals 8000 grams using place value. In the Customary U.S. system the patterns are not as automatic, but each unit is still scaled up proportionally using multiplication, or scaled down as the case may require.

MATHEMATICAL MODELING

Initially models emerge as a representation *of* a situation; later they are used by teachers to represent children's computation strategies. Ultimately they are appropriated by children as powerful tools *for* thinking (Gravemeijer, 1999). Two models are used in *Muffles' Measurement Models (Parts 1 and 2)*: the double number line and the ratio table.

❖ Model of a situation

The double open number line model is introduced as a representation of the equivalence of linear units of distance. This is a powerful model for exploring grouping, unitizing, and equivalence. The model encourages a linear representation of numbers and number operations for children that is powerful for developing mental arithmetic strategies (Beishuizen 1993; Klein, Beishuizen, and Treffers 2002). The line can represent the measurement tools showing both the unit and the grouping: the meter stick shows the centimeters and decimeters to support grouping, equivalence, and the algebraic strategy of substituting an equivalent expression. Using models like this supports converting from one unit to another effectively. See the figure below:

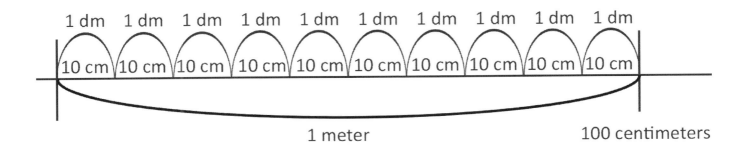

A second model used in both units is the ratio table. The ratio table emerges as Muffles' Charts—charts that help Patricio with Muffles' recipes and other needed conversions.

Liters	Deciliters	Centiliters
1	10	100
2	20	200
½	5	50
1 ½	15	150

The ratio table supports children to think proportionally, to use partial products, and to scale up or down keeping the rates constant.

❖ Model of Students' Strategies

Children benefit from seeing the teacher model their strategies. Once the model has been introduced as a representation of the situation, you can use it to model children's strategies as they convert. Notes are provided within the unit to help you do this.

❖ Model as a Tool for Thinking

Eventually children will be able to use the open double number line and the ratio table as tools—for thinking about measurement, and about multiplication and division in general. They will be able to imagine number as measurements on a number line and mentally mark lengths (and jumps) in various configurations. They will understand how equivalent length sections can be exchanged and the strategy of exchanging equivalent sections will become automatic. They will also have become skilled measurers: measuring competently, knowing the need for identical units and consistent relationships between units, knowing how to partition units into smaller equal parts, and knowing how to convert fluently. They will be able to employ proportional reasoning using a ratio table, which in time will become a powerful tool for representing input/output, linear functions, and even the graphing of points as Cartesian coordinates.

Lastly, note the difference between additive and multiplicative structuring. Early in development when children are using strategies based on skip counting and/or repeated addition they are modeling the problem additively. When they begin to scale and use proportional reasoning a major shift has occurred. They are now modeling the problem multiplicatively. Another example of additive structuring is finding that 3 meters = 30 decimeters by adding 10 + 10 + 10. In contrast, multiplicative structuring would be scaling and immediately using place value patterns: 3 meters = 30 decimeters = 300 centimeters, etc.

A graphic of the full landscape of learning for systems of measurement is provided on page 10. The purpose of the graphic is to allow you to see the longer journey of students' measurement development and to place your work with these two companion units within the scope of this long-term development. You may also find the graphic helpful as a way to record the progress of individual students for yourself. Each landmark can be shaded in as you find evidence in a student's work and in what the student says—evidence that a landmark strategy, big idea, or way of modeling has been constructed. Or, you may prefer to use our web-based app (www.NewPerspectivesOnAssessment.com) to document your children's growth digitally. In a very real sense, you will be recording the individual pathways your students take as they develop as young mathematicians.

References and Resources

Beishuizen, Meindert (1993). Mental strategies and materials or models for addition and subtraction up to 100 in Dutch second grades. *Journal for Research in Mathematics Education, 24,* 294–323.

Gravemeijer, Koeno (1999). How emergent models may foster the constitution of formal mathematics. *Mathematical Thinking and Learning 1* (2): 155–77.

Klein, Anton S., Meindert Beishuizen, and Adri Treffers. (2002). The empty number line in Dutch second grade, In *Lessons learned from research,* eds. Judith Sowder and Bonnie Schapelle. Reston, VA: NCTM.

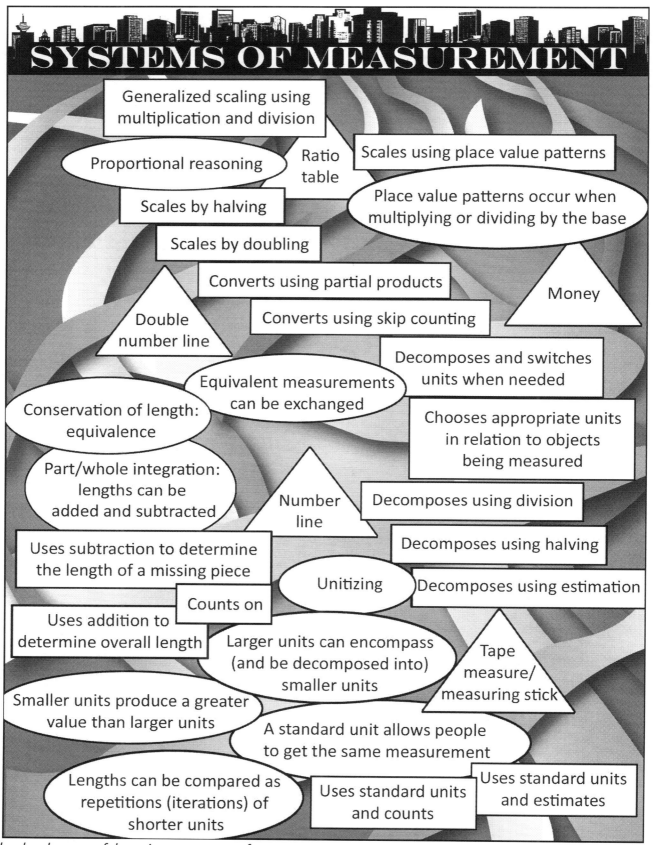

The landscape of learning: systems of measurement on the horizon showing landmark strategies (rectangles), big ideas (ovals), and models (triangles).

DAY ONE

PATRICIO'S LINE

Materials Needed

Muffles' Truffles Posters (Appendices A1 and A2)

How long is the line? (Appendix B)

The Meters Chart (Appendix C)

A trundle wheel (metric)

Pencils

Drawing paper or several sheets of copy paper

Blank Chart Paper for posters (sticky note style is best as it makes taping on the walls unnecessary)

Markers

This unit begins with the introduction (or re-introduction) of Muffles, a chocolatier. If you and your students have previously worked through the unit *Muffles' Truffles* or *Muffles' Measurement Models: Customary U.S. Units (Part One)*, the character won't be new to your students. But for others, Muffles and his truffles shop will be a new context. It is not necessary to have done the earlier units.

Like Part One, this unit has measurement as its goal, but this time the focus is on place value and the metric system. Muffles decides to open a second shop in Ottawa, Ontario because of the popularity of his truffles. He sends Patricio to Canada to help the new proprietor open up. Patricio is faced with an unfamiliar measurement system in Canada: the metric system. How will he ever measure customer lines to place the wait signs, or help the new proprietor with recipe charts?

Day One Outline

Developing the Context
- ❖ Tell the story of Muffles and his shop using Appendices A1 and A2.
- ❖ Facilitate a discussion on the metric system and what tool might be best for Patricio to use to measure for the signs.
- ❖ Continue the story using Appendix B and send students off in pairs to figure out the length of the line in centimeters, meters, kilometers, and dekameters.

Supporting the Investigation
- ❖ Confer with children as they work, noting the strategies they use and how they convert.
- ❖ Support students to note that as the units of measure increase in size, the amount of units needed decreases, and the arithmetic becomes easier. Encourage them to explain why.
- ❖ As students finish, ask them to prepare a poster to convince others of their solutions and important things they have noticed. These posters will be used on Day Two in a gallery walk and congress.

Developing the Context

Appendix A1 provides a picture of Muffles that you can use to introduce (or re-introduce) him to your class as you tell the following story:

> **Tech Tip**
>
> To develop the context, many teachers take a photo of Appendix A with a cell phone or iPad and project it. Others use a document camera to project the page onto a whiteboard or screen.

Muffles is a chocolatier who has a small, but very popular, truffles shop in the U.S. He makes truffles and packages them in boxes of ten. When he first opened his shop, he had only a few customers—his family and friends. His truffles were so delicious, so delectable, that soon his customers couldn't stop eating them. They also couldn't stop talking about the most delicious truffles in the world. They told their friends, who in turn told their friends, who in turn told their friends, and before Muffles knew it he had so many customers he could hardly keep up with the demand for truffles. Long lines of people waited outside his door; sometimes the line even snaked around the corner. Sometimes there were so many customers that Muffles ran out of truffles. What sad faces! What disappointment! But Muffles' assistant, Patricio, had come to the rescue. He had put signs along the line where the customers were waiting telling them the approximate wait time and he had made new recipe charts so Muffles could make really big batches of truffles.

One day a customer named Pierre asked Muffles if he had ever considered opening up another shop, in another city. Pierre was from Ottawa, the capitol city of Canada. Pierre explained that he was also a chocolatier and that he thought Muffles' truffles were the best he had ever had, and if Muffles' was interested in opening up another shop in Ottawa, he would like to be the new proprietor. Muffles loved the idea! Another shop! And, in Ottawa!

Muffles told Patricio about the new shop and asked him to fly up and help Pierre get the new shop ready. Patricio was very excited. He had never been to Ottawa, or even Canada for that matter. Now he would get to travel and see a new part of the world. Muffles had trusted him with a big job getting the new shop ready, but Patricio felt ready and up to it. After all, he had helped Muffles with some hard jobs, too. He had measured the line of customers for a reporter's story on the shop; he had built a model to determine where signs should go telling customers how much more time they had to wait in line to get to the counter; and he had helped Muffles make recipe charts for bigger batches of the most popular truffles. Patricio took off for the airport feeling very confident and excited.

When he arrived in Ottawa, Patricio found his way to the shop easily. The cab driver knew exactly where the address was. The shop was on a very busy street in the middle of the downtown shopping district. "Oh boy," Patricio thought to himself, "Pierre is going to have a very long line of customers in this neighborhood, much longer than Muffles' line even!

I will need to measure carefully and put a lot of signs up for customers so they know how long the wait will be to get to the counter, just like I did for Muffles," Patricio thought. He set straight to work. He asked Pierre for a big tape measure, the longest he had, and said he would mark out the yards. Pierre explained that in Canada and pretty much around the world the metric system is used to measure distance, not feet and yards.

[Show Appendix A2 as you continue with the story]

"The metric system..? Which tool should I use?" asked Patricio.

"I've got a really good tool for you that will make the job easy," said Pierre. "This is called a trundle wheel and it measures 1 meter around. It has a clicker and all you have to do is walk with it on the ground. Let it roll. Each roll is a meter. It clicks when it goes around once so all you have to do is count the clicks. Roll it 100 times and make a mark. We'll plan on putting a sign there. Do that five times and I'll make 5 signs."

Patricio set to work. He rolled the trundle wheel down the street watching the wheel go around. He counted the clicks very carefully and when he got to 100 he made a mark. He did this five times just as Pierre had told him. When he was done he had made a very long line down the street and around a few blocks and it had 5 small marks for the signs. "How long is this line?" Patricio wondered.

Teacher Note

If you don't have access to a trundle wheel, you can find and print or project images that will help students visualize the tool Patricio is using.

Patricio knew that whenever he had a challenging math problem it always helped to model it, so he drew a line and made 5 ticks on it. Under the first tick he wrote 100 meters. "Will this model help me?" Patricio wondered. "What should I do next?"

Pass out Appendices B and C (one copy of each to each pair of students). Ensure that children understand the picture of the line on Appendix B and how it depicts what Patricio did with the trundle wheel. Assign math partners and send students off to investigate. Provide drawing paper and pencils in case students wish to redraw the line and use it as a tool as they work.

Supporting the Investigation

As students begin to work, note first with a quick look around if all students are engaged and understand the context. Work first to ensure students understand the context—what Patricio did with the trundle wheel and how he modeled the problem—and then sit and confer with a few pairs as they work.

If any students complain that they don't know how to start, you might remind them that mathematicians often start by trying to model the problem. Ask if they think Patricio's model might be helpful. See what ideas they have for using it and ask what they think Patricio would do next.

Many students may write equivalent ratios on the line shown on Appendix B, for example 100 meters on the bottom of the line and 10,000 centimeters on the top. Then they may skip count and reach a ratio of ½ kilometer = 500 meters = 50,000 centimeters. See what students do with the dekameter and decimeter. Often students note that the chart (Appendix C) says the dekameter is 10 times the meter and they quickly write 1,000 dekameters above the 100 meters. This is a moment not to be missed because a big idea is at play here. If the tool is 10 times longer than the meter, then the number of meters needs to be divided by 10 to determine the number of dekameters, not multiplied by 10. On the other hand, when the unit is 10 times smaller than the meter (decimeter), there will be 10 times the number of meters because 10 decimeters fit in each meter. Get children discussing this idea and don't be afraid to foster puzzlement. Provide time for them to discuss and reflect on this relationship. Disequilibrium engenders learning!

Behind the Numbers

The metric system is built on scaling up and down by ten. If students are comfortable with multiplication and division by ten, they may easily note the patterns produced. But there is still opportunity here for rich discussions. Ask students why the pattern of putting the zero on the end when you multiply by ten happens. Facilitate the discussion to help them realize that 10 hundreds is also 100 tens (10x100 = 100x10). In the number 1,000, help them see the 10 hundreds (10 is the two digits on the left) and the 100 tens (from the three digits on the left). Our place value system is beautiful; you can divide and multiply by the base by just moving to the left or to the right.

Inside One Classroom: Conferring with students at work

Catherine (the teacher): Hi Amy and Pauline. I've been looking at what you have been doing and I am fascinated by your strategy. Can I sit and confer with you on it?

Amy and Pauline: Sure! *(Both girls show genuine pleasure, beaming from the compliment.)*

Catherine: Well let me start by making sure I understand your strategy, OK? It looks to me like you are trying to do the dekameters, and you multiplied by 10?

Amy: Yep, because it says 10 times larger than the meter.

Catherine: Oh I see that now! But is the tool 10 times larger than the meter? Or is the answer 10 times larger? Let's try to use a line like Patricio did. If this is a meter would 10 dekameters fit in it, or would I need 10 of them to make a dekameter? *(Now both girls are thinking hard.)*

Author's notes

Catherine moves around the room, noting the strategies being used, and then sits to confer with a few groups as they work.

She starts the conferral by clarifying what the children

Pauline: Maybe inside, oh...oh no...the dekameter is 10 times bigger so the number has to be smaller.

Catherine: What do you think Amy?

Amy: So if it is 100 meters to this line, then 10 dekameters could get there too? We could just say 10 dekameters and write that on the top of the line above the 100 meters?

Catherine: Well, convince us. What do you think, Amy?

Amy: You could, because the wheel would have to go around 10 times to make a dekameter. And if it does that 10 times it would be 10 tens, so 100 meters.

Catherine: This is so exciting thinking about the turn of the trundle wheel! You have to get this on your poster for our gallery walk tomorrow! So what happens with the decimeter, and how is that different from the dekameter? I'll check back with you later and you can let me know, ok?

have done. Before she sat down she already had a good idea of the strategy they were using. She challenges them to think about the wheel. This move "ups the ante," but in a very supportive way. The role of the teacher is not to just facilitate; it is to mentor.

As she leaves to confer with other pairs at work, Catherine urges the girls to make sure they get that idea on their poster. This idea will be an important focus in the congress tomorrow.

As students begin to reach conclusions about how long the line is, ask them to prepare posters presenting their findings for a gallery walk and congress on Day Two. Explain that mathematicians often want to share their findings with each other, and that when they do they are careful to choose the most important ideas to share. As students prepare their work on poster paper, they should not copy every step they took. Instead, encourage students to record how their thinking changed, the interesting connections they noticed, and the arguments they used to convince each other that their answers were correct. How did they convert from one unit to another? What did they notice along the way that might have made their work easier?

Reflections on the Day

Today students were asked to measure length, and to convert within the metric system: from meters to centimeters to kilometers. The double number line can be used as a helpful tool in converting from one unit to another. The model supports the use of ratio thinking and using it saves a lot of arithmetic! It also supports children to use multiplicative structuring instead of additive structuring. It supports them to scale up and down by ten. Along the way students most likely came to realize that as the unit used became bigger, the number of times they needed to iterate it was proportionately smaller. Day Two's congress will provide an opportunity for a rich discussion about ways to convert from one unit to another and how using larger units makes the numbers smaller and can require far less work! There will likely also be some nice discussion on multiplication and division by ten, and the place value patterns that result.

DAY TWO

HOW LONG IS THE LINE?

Materials Needed

Students' work from Day One

Markers and Pencils

Sticky notes (about 3 per student)

Today begins with a minilesson as a warm-up to math workshop. Students work with a string of related problems designed to support further ratio thinking in converting from one unit to another. After the minilesson, finishing touches are put to posters and a gallery walk ensues to provide students with opportunities to read and write viable arguments—an important standard of mathematical practice. After the gallery walk a congress is held to discuss a few of the pieces more deeply.

Day Two Outline

Minilesson: A String of Related Problems
❖ Work on a string of related problems designed to encourage students to convert fluently using multiplicative structuring.

Facilitating the Gallery Walk
❖ Confer with children as they put finishing touches to their posters, asking them to consider the most important things they want to tell their audience about smart ways to convert.
❖ Conduct a gallery walk to allow students time to reflect and comment on each other's posters from Day One.

Facilitating the Math Congress
❖ Convene students at the meeting area to discuss a few important ideas about converting from one unit of measure to another, such as the fact that the bigger the unit used the fewer iterations are needed. Examine how some strategies required a great deal of arithmetic while others didn't.

Minilesson: A String of Related Problems

This string is designed to help students use multiplicative structuring, more flexibly converting one unit to another using strategies based on ratio thinking and place value. Represent the problems on a t-chart like the one below, one problem at a time, moving from the top to the bottom of the chart, and invite students to share their conversion strategies. As they do, record their thinking on the t-chart.

The String:

	Meters	Decimeters	Centimeters
1 meter	1		
2 meters	2		
100 decimeters		100	
50 decimeters		50	
40 decimeters		40	
900 centimeters			900
1600 centimeters			1600
8 meters	8		

Behind the Numbers

The first problem is a helper requiring only the knowledge given the day before: 1 meter equals 10 decimeters, which equal 100 centimeters. You can use a trundle wheel to show how there are decimeters and centimeters on the wheel. Or, if you don't have one, use a meter stick. As you move through the string many relations will surface such as doubling, halving, and partial products. But the use of the place value (multiplication and division by ten) will likely be the easiest. Encourage children to note the relations and explain why the "zero trick" works by focusing on the commutative property (see p. 5). Help them generalize what happens when you multiply and divide by ten.

Facilitating the Gallery Walk

Ask students to return to the posters they began on Day One, adding any finishing touches they desire. As they work, move around and confer asking them to consider the most important things they want to tell their audience about smart ways to convert. Remind them that it is not necessary to write about everything they did, but instead to concentrate on convincing their audience about the important things they discovered and want to defend. Depending on how much prior experience your students have had doing gallery walks, it may be helpful to provide instructions before you pass out the sticky notes. If your students have not done a gallery walk for some time, or if you think they need more instruction on how to proceed, see the Teacher Note section below.

Teacher Note

Let your students know that their comments and questions should be specific about the math on the poster, and to steer clear of comments such as "Good job!" or "I like your poster." Remind students that mathematicians write proofs. They defend their ideas to convince other mathematicians that they are right. Thus, specific comments and questions are most helpful. It may help to give the example of writing workshop, since most students can remember a time when a peer said something like, "I like your story!" but did not explain why. Once you have gone over a few examples and perhaps even modeled writing a comment or question, pass out the sticky notes. Explain that you are going to start by passing out three sticky notes, and students can return to get more if needed.

Ask students to start at different places and choose just three or four posters to focus on. Remind them to read carefully and then give each poster a few sticky notes, enough so that after about ten minutes, all posters will have at least a few comments. Remind students that gallery walks should be quiet times so that all reviewers can read and think before commenting. This time should be taken seriously. One of the Standards of Mathematical Practice is to read and write viable arguments and this is a time to foster the development of that ability.

After the gallery walk, invite the groups to go back to their posters to see what comments and questions were left. Allow a few minutes for everyone to think about the feedback they received and to discuss any new ideas with their partners before convening the whole class in the meeting area for a congress.

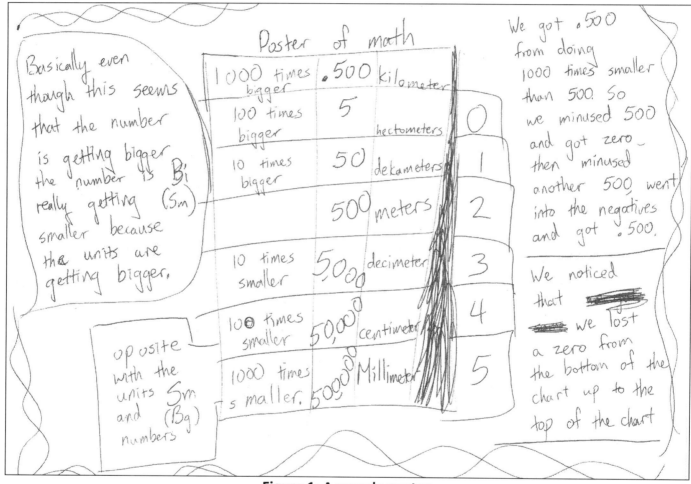

Figure 1: A sample poster

Facilitating the Congress

Review the posters and choose a few that you can use for a discussion that will deepen understanding and support growth along the landscape of learning described in the overview. There is not necessarily one best plan for a congress. There are many different plans that might all be supportive of development.

If your school has purchased P2S2™, the support system for CFLM (www.NewPerspectivesOnline.net), you will find many tips on it about how to plan congresses. For example, you might start with a sample pair that used skip counting by 100, or repeated addition (an example of additive structuring), tediously working to get a total of the number of meters first. If the pair used a model and then marked the other units on it, the piece might serve as a focus for a discussion on the power of drawing a model and using it as a tool for thinking. Starting the congress with a work sample like this will also serve as a support for other students who may have generated the idea that the bigger the unit, the fewer units needed.

A second nice choice might be a piece by a pair that started by converting the measurement of the first marker: 100 meters = 10 dekameters = 1,000 decimeters = 10,000 centimeters. Here you can ask everyone to step back and look for any patterns in the numbers that they might see. Support them to notice the place value relationships.

Lastly, use a poster like the one shown in Figure 1 that shows the use of 5 x 100 meters to get the length of the line. Now only place value is needed: 500 meters is 0.5 or ½ a kilometer, or 5 hectometers, 50 dekameters, 5,000 decimeters, etc. Thinking like this is a beautiful example of multiplicative structuring because of the flexible scaling up and scaling down using proportional reasoning and multiplication and division by ten. It is a nice piece of work to use for a discussion on how one can move to the right when multiplying by ten, and to the left when dividing by ten.

Whatever pieces you decide to use make sure that one of the big ideas discussed is that the bigger the units used when measuring, the smaller the number of iterations. Since a dekameter is 10 times bigger than the meter, the answer will be 10 times smaller, but the measurements are equivalent.

Inside One Classroom: A portion of the congress

Catherine (the teacher): We started math workshop with a minilesson and discussed how taking one measurement and multiplying or dividing it by 10 could be helpful with others. I noticed during our gallery walk how many of you found interesting ways to calculate the length of the line by doing just that. And different people used different points on Patricio's model to do that. Let's look at a few together and let's see what we came up with. Sally and Ben, would you start us off and explain your approach?

Sally: Well, we noticed that the trundle wheel that Patricio used had 100 centimeters on it, so every time the wheel did a meter, it also did 100 centimeters.

Ben: Yeah. See...where Patricio had written 100 meters, we also wrote 10,000 centimeters.

Catherine: Interesting! Let's turn and talk with a shoulder partner. See if your partner knows what Ben and Sally did.

Author's notes

Catherine starts the congress with a piece of work that makes use of the number line model. For children who still need to mark each line, for example those that are still skip counting, it provides an entry point.

Pair talk is provided to discuss what the group has done and to give time to reflect on it.

(After a few minutes of pair talk, Catherine resumes whole group discussion.) Who has a question or comment for Ben and Sally?

Noah: How did you know what numbers to put with the dekameter and the decimeter? We got mixed up on those. The chart said 10 times bigger and so we made the answer 10 times bigger. But it wasn't, it was 10 times smaller.

Ben: That's because the tool is 10 times bigger than the meter. It takes 10 meters to even make 1 dekameter.

Noah: Oh, I get it! But then how did you figure out the decimeters?

Ben: The decimeter tool is 10 times smaller than the meter. There's 10 decimeters in a meter, so in a 100 meters there is 10x100.

Catherine: Who agrees? *(Lots of hands go up.)* Turn and explain it to your partner. See if they need help understanding it.

Discussion is not possible without the majority of the group understanding the strategy. The pair talk supports others to now ask questions. It is important to get the conversation going back and forth between the students rather than teacher/ kid/ teacher.

Now Ben's explanation makes more sense. Catherine's goal is accomplished: the community is being requested to consider scaling by 10, and to understand the relationship and proportional reasoning (if the tool is 10 times bigger, then the answer is a value 10 times smaller).

Reflections on the Day

Math workshop began today with a minilesson where students were supported to convert making use of the relationships in a t-chart. The minilesson may have supported your students to refine their thinking as they prepared for the gallery walk. By participating in a gallery walk on their work from Day One, students had opportunities to read and write viable arguments and then consider their classmates' comments, questions, and suggestions. Opportunities like these are designed to support the development of proof-making. A math congress provided opportunities for further discussion and reflection on the topic of measurement conversion and by the end of the day you are likely already noticing how several of your students are starting to think proportionally.

DAY THREE

PATRICIO'S MODEL

Materials Needed

Patricio's Model (Appendix D, one copy per pair of students)

Pencils

Drawing paper or several sheets of copy paper

Blank Chart Paper for posters (sticky note style is best as it makes taping on the walls unnecessary)

Markers

Today begins with a minilesson as a warm-up to math workshop. Students work with a string of related problems designed to support further ratio thinking in converting from one unit to another. After the minilesson a new context is presented. Patricio shows Pierre the model he made for Muffles showing the time customers would have to wait. Now he needs to put up signs for Pierre. Pierre has made five signs and on each he has written how far away the shop is. On the last one he has written ½ kilometer; on the next 400 meters, then 300 meters, etc. Patricio needs to add information to the signs so customers can tell how long the wait is as they are standing in line. How can he figure this out, and what should he put on the signs: seconds, minutes, or hours?

Day Three Outline

Minilesson: A String of Related Problems
❖ Work on a string of related problems designed to encourage students to convert fluently using multiplicative structuring.

Developing the Context
❖ Tell the story of Patricio's Experiment using Appendix D.
❖ Facilitate a discussion on how Patricio's model might be helpful and ask students to finish the chart on Appendix D.

Supporting the Investigation
❖ Confer with children as they work, noting the strategies they use and how they convert.
❖ As students finish, ask them to prepare a poster to convince others of their solutions and important things they have noticed along the way as they worked. These posters will be used on Day Four in a gallery walk and congress.

Minilesson: A String of Related Problems

This string is designed in a similar fashion to the one you used on Day Two. Its purpose is to help students use multiplicative structuring to convert more flexibly from one unit to another, using strategies based on ratio thinking and place value patterns. Represent the problems on a t-chart like the one below, one problem at a time, moving from the top to the bottom of the chart, and invite students to share their conversion strategies. As they do, record their thinking on the t-chart.

Centimeters	Decimeters	Meters
		1
		2
		3
		9
		10
		5
		19

Behind the Numbers

The first problem is a helper requiring only the knowledge given the day before: 1 meter equals 10 decimeters, which equal 100 centimeters. 2 meters are double the first row, and so are the centimeters and decimeters. To determine 3 meters, 1 meter and 2 meters can be combined. 9 meters is triple the 3 meters and 10 is just 1 meter more. 5 meters is half of 10 so the centimeters and decimeters are halved as well. 19 may be difficult for some but encourage them to look for pieces they know, for example that 10 and 9 can be added to produce partial products. What is likely to happen though is that students will see how easy it is to just go across the row to the left and use multiplication by 10 and 100! And how nice that they do—they are seeing the beauty of our place value system.

Developing the Context

Project a copy of Appendix D if you have the technology to do so, and read the story on it as you develop the context. If you don't have the technology, just pass out Appendix D so that each pair of students has a copy and read the story on it to them. Remember to develop it in an exciting way to engage them in the story. Make the context come alive!

Discuss the context to make sure students understand Patricio's model, also ensuring they understand that Patricio used 3 meters, 6 people fit in that distance, and he knew 6 people would take 10 minutes because he had done an experiment for Muffles a long time ago.

Some students will likely comment that some customers might take longer and Patricio can't assume that every 10 minutes 6 people will get to the counter. Of course this is true. Acknowledge that it is a good point, but remind students of the situation. Patricio needs to place signs that show average times so customers can judge whether they want to wait or not. Point out that in the first group of 6 people that took 10 minutes there might have been some customers who were quick and others who took longer, too. You can also say that often mathematicians have to decide ahead on certain assumptions they will use when they set out to mathematize a problem. As a community it is important to use the same assumptions or it is difficult to compare solutions. Patricio's model assumes 3 meters for 6 people and that takes about 10 minutes. Suggest that as a community this rate be the one used to finish Patricio's model, since it is the rate he started with, then send them off in pairs to finish the model and work on the questions on Appendix D. Remind them that they have drawing paper, too, if they want to redraw the model to help them.

Supporting the Investigation

The drawing of the line with the marks and a ratio table are provided again on purpose as they may potentially generate a strategy of proportional reasoning. For example, some students might skip count by 3 meters. If they proceed this way they might notice that 6 meters take 20 minutes and 9 meters take ½ hour. If they do notice this they now have a nice ratio they can use: 18 meters will take 60 minutes, or 1 hour.

Some may calculate the number of people first: 6 people in each group and 5 groups (only 30 people are shown). If 6 people take 10 minutes, it will take 50 minutes for the last of the 30 people to get to the counter. Six more people would take another 10 minutes, so 36 people in line would take an hour. Other students may recognize that if there are 60 minutes in an hour, each group of 6 will take 10 minutes, or 1/6 of an hour.

There are many strategies that can be used to solve the problem and Patricio's model should be a helpful one to support movement from skip counting and/or tedious arithmetic strategies to the use of scaling. Confer with children as they work, noting the strategies they use as they scale up and convert. Do they add, skip count, or use partial products? As you confer support students to use more flexible strategies than they used on Day One and celebrate with them the advances you see in their approaches.

Be prepared that some students may represent the minutes as a portion of an hour in a variety of ways and as you confer keep an eye out for this. For example, take a look at the samples of work in Figure 2.

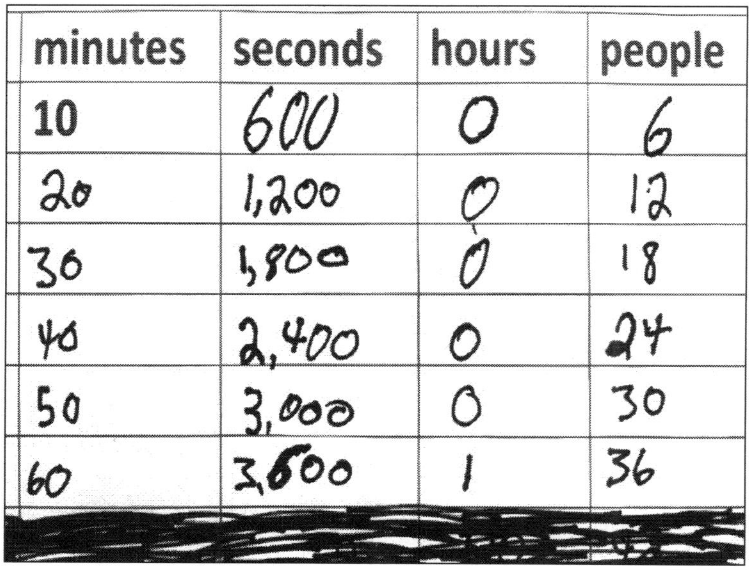

minutes	seconds	hours	people
10	600	0	6
20	1,200	0	12
30	1,800	0	18
40	2,400	0	24
50	3,000	0	30
60	3,600	1	36

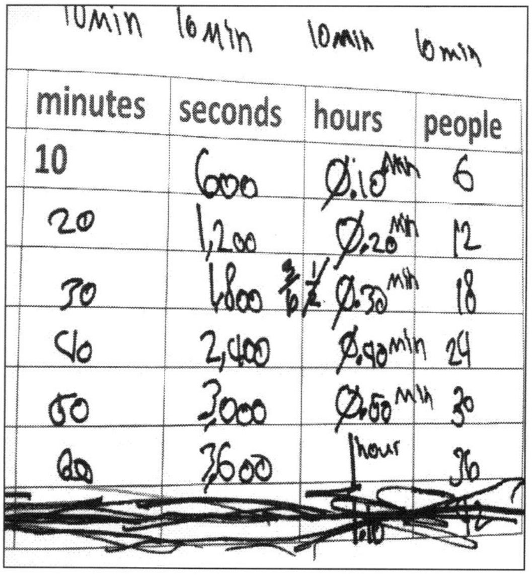

10min 10min 10min 10min

minutes	seconds	hours	people
10	600	0.10 min	6
20	1,200	0.20 min	12
30	1800	0.30 min	18
40	2,400	0.40 min	24
50	3000	0.50 min	30
60	3600	1 hour	36

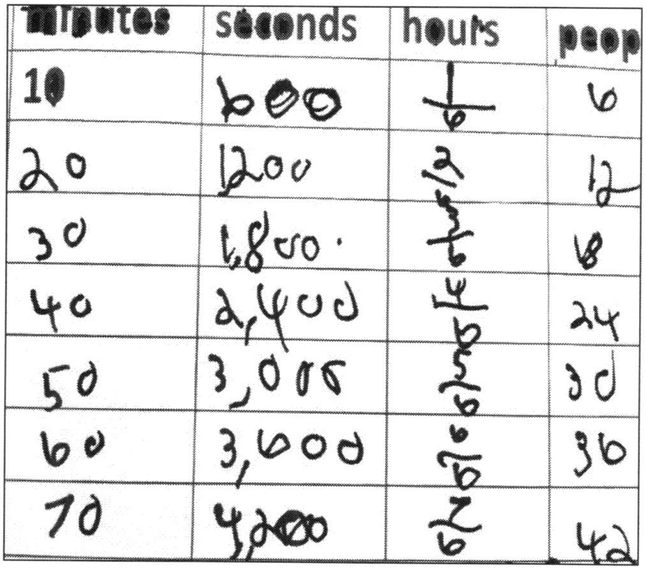

minutes	seconds	hours	peop
10	600	1/6	6
20	1200	2/6	12
30	1,800	3/6	18
40	2,400	4/6	24
50	3,000	5/6	30
60	3,600	6/6	36
70	4200	7/6	42

Figure 2: Three Samples of Student Work

The first piece makes no attempt to show the minutes as a portion of the whole hour. It is important to get your students to consider what portion of the hour 10 minutes is. It is true there is not a complete hour yet, but there is a portion of an hour. Encourage students to examine how many 10-minute portions there are in an hour and establish the equivalence: 10 minutes = 1/6 of an hour. This is the thinking that is evident in the third sample. It represents thinking of the 10 minutes as 1 part out of 6 parts: 10 minutes x 6 = 60 minutes. Note how the second piece of work attempts to show the minutes using decimal notation. Students will often do this so keep a look out for it. They are not considering the decimals as ratios representing a portion of the whole broken into hundredths. The hour does not have 100 minutes in it, only 60. Ten minutes is 10/60 of an hour, not 10/100.

As students finish, ask them to prepare a poster to convince others of their solutions and important things they have noticed along the way as they worked. These posters will be used on Day Four in a gallery walk and congress.

Reflections on the Day

Math workshop began today again with a minilesson where students were supported to convert making use of the relationships in a t-chart. The minilesson may have supported your students to make use of scaling and partial products and you may have seen these strategies carrying over when students worked on Patricio's model. As you moved around and conferred you may have noticed also that more and more students are starting to use ratio thinking. The movement from skip counting to scaling is huge as it requires a shift from additive structuring to multiplicative structuring—to thinking proportionally. You are witnessing major development in front of your eyes and it is important to document it. Take a look at the landscape in the overview. Have you seen your children traversing the landscape? Continue to document each child's journey along it. You can highlight each child's path on the graphic of the landscape provided in the overview of this unit. There is an app available to do so as well if you wish to capture and document your students' development digitally (www.NewPerspectivesOnAssessment.com).

DAY FOUR

HOW LONG A WAIT?

Materials Needed

Students' work from Day Three

Markers and Pencils

Sticky notes (about 3 per student)

Today begins with students adding finishing touches to posters from Day Three and a gallery walk ensues. After the gallery walk a congress is held to discuss a few of the pieces more deeply. The congress ends with a minilesson. Students work with a string of related problems designed to support further ratio thinking in converting from one unit to another.

Day Four Outline

Facilitating the Gallery Walk
- Confer with children as they put finishing touches to their posters, asking them to consider the most important things they want to tell their audience about smart ways to convert.
- Conduct a gallery walk to allow students time to reflect and comment on each other's posters.

Facilitating the Math Congress
- Convene students at the meeting area to discuss a few important ideas about converting from one unit of measure to another, and how Patricio's model was helpful.

Minilesson: A String of Related Problems
- Work on a string of related problems designed to encourage students to convert fluently using multiplicative structuring.

Facilitating the Gallery Walk

Ask students to return to the posters they began on Day Three, adding any finishing touches they desire. As they work, move around and confer, asking them to consider the most important things they want to tell their audience about smart ways to convert. Remind them that it is not necessary to write about everything they did, but instead to concentrate on convincing their audience about the important things they discovered and want to defend.

The main purpose of a gallery walk is of course the development of the reading and writing of viable arguments, but a secondary purpose is to provide time for reflection, refinement, and consolidation of the thinking learners generated as they investigated the problem. Often when students are postering, the ideas they write about go beyond what they actually did. Students may have started with just skip counting strategies or doing a great deal of arithmetic, but as they worked they might have had an insight on a more efficient strategy. In particular they may have moved from additive structuring to a more multiplicative way of thinking, for example doubling or scaling. They should focus their posters on the latter, as this is an insight they had that is an important idea to share. Encouraging students to just write about what they did may not be as supportive of development as encouraging them to write about an insight they had as they worked and to write a convincing argument about it. As you move around conferring and helping your students to get ready for the gallery walk, look for moments where you can facilitate development—moments where you can support scaling and other more efficient strategies based on place value.

Ask students to start at different places and choose three or four posters to focus on. Remind them to read carefully and then give each poster a few sticky notes, enough so that after about ten minutes, all posters will have at least a few comments. Remind students that gallery walks should be quiet times so that all reviewers can read and think before commenting. This time should be taken seriously.

During the gallery walk it's important that you make comments on posters as well. It's important that students see you as a member of the community, not someone grading their papers, so look for moments and places where you can show them you are seriously trying to understand their thinking. Make your comments as a member of the audience, suggesting where more detail could be helpful to support understanding and commenting on interesting approaches. Raise questions that might push for generalization. As you move around look for big ideas and strategies from the landscape. This is a nice time also to plan which pieces of work you will select for the congress.

Facilitating the Math Congress

Review the posters and choose a few that you can use for a discussion that will deepen understanding and support growth along the landscape of learning described in the overview.

There is not necessarily one best plan for a congress. There are many different plans that might all be supportive of development. You'll want to make this congress supportive of the use of the ratio table as a tool: jumping around on it in clever ways for converting and using equivalent rates. But remember to work developmentally. If you start with an approach that shows a strong understanding of scaling for example, but one that will be difficult for most of your students to understand, you will lose many during the discussion. Think about how to scaffold your congress so that entry levels exist for those who aren't thinking multiplicatively yet. Think about how you might connect the strategies you use so that the discussion that occurs actually promotes new insights.

> **Tech Tip**
>
> You might take pictures of students' work using an iPad and project them onto a whiteboard or smart board. When different ideas come up in discussions, revisions can be drawn without having to mark on the student's work. Apps such as *Adobe Sketch* or *Explain Everything* can be useful tools for this.

Minilesson: A String of Related Problems

This string is designed to continue helping students use multiplicative structuring and place value patterns, more flexibly converting one unit to another using strategies based on proportional reasoning and multiplication and division by ten. Doing it after the congress instead of at the beginning of math workshop is beneficial because the congress most likely supported the ability to scale and this gives students a chance to practice what they were discussing.

Represent the problems on a t-chart like the one below, one problem at a time, moving from the top to the bottom of the chart, and invite students to share their conversion strategies. As they do, record their thinking on the t-chart.

The String:

Meters	Centimeters	Time
3	300	10 minutes
	600	
	150	
	1500	
30		
		1 hour
	2100	

600 centimeters
150 centimeters
1500 centimeters
30 meters
1 hour
2100 centimeters

Behind the Numbers

600 is double the 300, and 150 is half of the 300. To get the meters the 3 can be halved resulting in 1½ or 1.5. The minutes are 5 (half of the 10). 1500 can be solved by scaling using place value. 1500 centimeters = 15 meters. 30 meters may also be able to be seen as 3000 centimeters. The time is now 100 minutes, or 1 hour and 40 minutes. The next two problems provide for several partial product strategies: 1 hour is 10 minutes plus 50 minutes, so 300 plus 1500 produces 1800 centimeters or 18 meters. 2100 centimeters is 1 hour (1800 cm) plus 10 minutes (300 cm).

Reflections on the Day

Math workshop began today with preparation for a gallery walk. As you moved around and conferred you may have noticed that more and more students are now starting to use ratio thinking. Each day you should see your children making progress on the landscape, but each child's pathway will likely be different. The lessons are not designed with one goal for all—one "it" for everyone to get. Each child should be learning, but most likely they are not all learning the same thing. Learning *is* development. The movement from skip counting to scaling is huge as it requires a shift from additive structuring to multiplicative structuring—to thinking proportionally. You are witnessing major development in front of your eyes. Document the journey!

DAY FIVE

MUFFLES' RECIPES

Materials Needed

Muffles' Recipes (Appendix E, one per student)

The Grams and Liters Charts (Appendices F and G, one per pair of students)

Pencils

Drawing paper or several sheets of copy paper

Blank Chart Paper for posters (sticky note style is best as it makes taping on the walls unnecessary)

Markers

Today begins with another minilesson designed to support multiplicative structuring and the flexible conversion of units of time, then a new context is developed. Patricio's next job is to work on charts for Muffles' recipes. In this investigation students are introduced to some new units: liters and grams. This context also uses a ratio table as a tool to support further scaling up and down and conversions to larger and smaller units. As students work to generate recipes for larger batches, many opportunities will occur for rich discussions on equivalence and proportional reasoning related to measurement.

Day Five Outline

Minilesson: A String of Related Problems
❖ Work on a string of related time problems designed to encourage students to convert fluently using multiplicative structuring.

Developing the Context
❖ Tell the story of Muffles' recipes and the units of measure he uses in making his truffles using Appendix E
❖ Facilitate a discussion on the equivalence of the units shown on Appendices F and G.
❖ Ask students to work in pairs on Appendix E, making a recipe chart for various batches of Muffles' dark chocolate truffles.

Supporting the Investigation
❖ Confer with children as they work, noting the strategies they use and how they convert.
❖ As students finish, ask them to prepare a poster to convince others of their solutions and important things they have noticed along the way as they worked. These posters will be used on Day Six in a gallery walk and congress.

Minilesson: A String of Related Problems

This string is designed in a similar fashion to the others you have been using all week. Its purpose, as with the others, is to keep familiarizing students with conversions. The focus today is on time. It also helps students use multiplicative structuring to convert more flexibly from one unit to another, using strategies based on proportional reasoning. Represent the problems on a t-chart like the one below, showing only one problem at a time, moving from the top to the bottom of the chart, and invite students to share their conversion strategies. As they do, record their thinking on the t-chart.

The String:

Seconds	Minutes	Hours
3600	60	1
		10
		2
		5
		9
		11
		6

Behind the Numbers

As students work to convert hours into seconds, the numbers will quickly become large. That is purposeful. The unwieldiness of trying to multiply each problem separately will cause students to consider the beauty of using other problems in the string and using strategies based on proportional reasoning. The first problem is a helper requiring only the knowledge given before: 1 hour = 60 minutes = 3600 seconds. The numbers are related in interesting ways to support the use of scaling and using partial products. As you work through the string you might not require students to do all of the arithmetic. Let them just tell you the strategies they would use so you can focus discussion on the relationships they see. For example, 9 hours can be solved as 600-60 minutes, and as 36,000-3,600 seconds. If you want to do the arithmetic, use an open number line model and remove helpful pieces: 3,6000 – 3,000 – 600.

Developing the Context

Use Appendices E, F, and G as you tell the following story. Remember to make the context come alive!

> *Patricio now turns to his next job—making the recipe charts. He calls Muffles and tells him he needs his basic recipes converted into the metric system. Muffles sends up his basic recipes all converted and Patricio sets off to make the new charts for the kitchen. He starts with the Dark Chocolate Truffles.*

Point out to the children that the basic recipe is in dekagrams and deciliters but as Muffles makes bigger batches he might want to use different units of measure to save time. Introduce the units listed on Appendices F and G, helping your students to understand the charts. Assign math partners and send students off to investigate what Patricio should write on his new charts.

> **Teacher Note: Behind the Numbers**
>
> The basic recipe proportions come from a standard truffles recipe. However, note that the basic recipe uses dekagrams and deciliters. As larger batches are made it makes more sense to measure with larger containers (units) and this provides students with the challenge of how best to convert.

Supporting the Investigation

As you move around conferring, take note of how children are moving on the table. Often, many students go across the top row first and when they get to the Very Big Batch they just assign a scaling factor randomly (for example 10 times the Big Batch, or 100 times the Basic Recipe, or 60 times the Big Batch perhaps from their work with the clock on Day Four). They also don't scale each ingredient by the same factor as they go down a column.

As you confer with students who do this, query them on why they picked the numbers they did. Suggest that they check the 4 liters of milk since it is on Muffles' chart already. How might they compare this with the 20 deciliters in the Big Batch? If they convert the 20 deciliters to 2 liters it's easy to determine that the Very Big Batch is just a double of the Big Batch.

If students do not use proportional reasoning consistently, you might ask, "If we increase the chocolate don't we need to increase the milk the same way? When you make chocolate milk if you don't put much chocolate in the milk what happens?" It's important to stay in the context to help children realize what they are doing. For an example of how to confer on this see the dialogue box from Inside One Classroom on page 33.

> **Teacher Note: Place Value Patterns**
>
> By this point, many students will see that it's just as easy to multiply by 100 or 1,000 as by 10. This is no accident. Multiplying by 100 (10x10) is like multiplying by 10^2, and 1,000 is like multiplying by 10^3, or by 10 three times. Numbers that are built by multiplying by ten, the powers of ten, each have their own place value in our number system and many also have individual prefixes in the metric system of measurement. When students "add" a zero place by placing it on the end of a number, or when they take it away to divide by 10, what they are actually doing is shifting the place value of the non-zero digits, making them 10 times larger or smaller. When students work with simple decimals later in this unit, the decimal point also becomes a tool for shifting place values: 0.5 is 10 times smaller than 5 and 0.05 is 100 times smaller. As students begin to build these connections, the place value relationships inherent in money can be a useful model to help them get started.

Inside One Classroom: Conferring with Students at Work

Catherine (the teacher): How are the three of you doing? May I sit and confer with you? *(The students all nod affirmatively and so Catherine continues.)* I see that you have written 36,000 truffles for the Very Big Batch. How did you get that number?

Josie: We multiplied the Big Batch by 600. See we wrote it down here. *(On their paper they have written 600 x 60 = 36,000.)*

Catherine: Yes, I see that now. But why 600? What made you decide to multiply by 600? Did you think this batch was 600 times bigger than the Basic Recipe? That's a lot of truffles! And I see that you then multiplied 2 deciliters by 60. I'm confused. How would you get 36,000 truffles, which you said was 600 times the Basic Recipe, if you only do 60 x 2 deciliters of milk? I'm also puzzled because it says 4 liters of milk for the Very Big Batch. Is that the same as the number of deciliters you got? Whew!! This is a real mystery, isn't it?

Josh: We could check the 4 liters...

Catherine: What a great idea! Go for it!

Josh: The Basic had 2 deciliters, so the double had 4, the triple had 6, and the quadruple had 8. The Big Batch is 10 times the basic so that is 20.

Catherine: I wonder if it would be helpful here to convert to liters. Remember on the other days how the bigger measurement units made the arithmetic easier because the numbers got smaller? I'm not sure, but it might help. What do you think?

Sasha: 20 deciliters is 2 liters. We could write that.

Catherine: Does this now help with the Very Big Batch?

Sasha: Oh! The Very Big Batch is double the Big Batch!

Catherine: This is so exciting! I think we've cracked part of the mystery! You have to get this on your poster for our gallery walk tomorrow! So if this recipe is double the Big Batch how many truffles will it make? I want to keep working with you, but I need to get to some other groups, too. I'll check back with you later and you can let me know, ok?

Author's notes

Catherine starts the conferral by clarifying what the children have done. Before she sat down she already had a good idea of the strategy they were using and she seeks in her next move to create disequilibrium. Intrigue can go a long way in helping kids develop the willingness to persevere—one of the important standards of mathematical practice. Then she supports by celebrating their next move.

Suggesting that they convert, is a way of reminding them of one of the big ideas in this unit: the larger the unit of measure, the smaller the total—and this makes the arithmetic easier.

As she leaves to confer with other pairs at work, Catherine urges the trio to make sure they get that idea on their poster. This idea will be an important focus in the congress tomorrow. Once again a celebration occurs. Note how it also feels to the children that Catherine is engaging in the inquiry with them. She even uses the pronoun "we." It's a conversation as she confers. It's not a test about what they know and where they made a mistake.

Reflections on the Day

Math workshop began today with another minilesson. Are the minilessons causing children to look for relationships and use them? If so, that is wonderful as they are making use of partial products and scaling. If not, reflect on how you might scaffold this more clearly during the discussion or perhaps repeat a string with a smaller group of children to allow everyone more space to reflect and be accountable for new ideas.

Remember that you can document children's growth on the landscape. You can copy or take pictures of each child's work and record your evidence on the landscape. And, even when this unit ends you can keep doing minilessons every day to continue working on multiplicative structuring and measurement conversions and record children's further progress. The investigation today was designed to introduce more units of measurement: this time for weight and liquid volume. As you moved around and conferred you may have noticed some children not scaling proportionately. Did you stay grounded in the context to help them? Did you find yourself asking, for example, if we only double the chocolate but use ten times the amount of milk would the batch be as chocolatey? Context will help children come to realize what they are doing. Without it, they can get lost in a world of numbers and have nothing to hang their hat on!

DAY SIX

MUFFLES' DARK CHOCOLATE TRUFFLES

Materials Needed

Students' work from Day Five

Markers and Pencils

Sticky notes (about 3 per student)

Today begins with students adding finishing touches to posters from Day Five and a gallery walk ensues. After the gallery walk a congress is held to discuss the relationship between the batches, the need to scale by the same factor, and the way the numbers change when converting between different units of weight and volume. The congress ends with a minilesson. Students work with a string of related problems designed to support further ratio thinking in converting from one measurement unit to another.

Day Six Outline

Facilitating the Gallery Walk
❖ Confer with children as they put finishing touches to their posters, asking them to consider the most important things they want to tell their audience about smart ways to convert.
❖ Conduct a gallery walk to allow students time to reflect and comment on each other's posters on the investigation started on Day Five.

Facilitating the Math Congress
❖ Convene students at the meeting area to discuss a few important ideas about converting efficiently from one unit of measure to another.

Minilesson: A String of Related Problems
❖ Work on a string of related problems designed to encourage students to convert fluently using multiplicative structuring.

Facilitating the Gallery Walk

Ask students to return to the posters they began on Day Five, adding any finishing touches they desire. As they work, move around and confer, asking them to consider the most important things they want to tell their audience about smart ways to convert. Remind them that it is not necessary to write about everything they did, but instead to concentrate on convincing their audience about the important things they discovered and want to defend.

Remember that during the gallery walk it's important that you make comments on posters as well. It's important that students see you as a member of the community, so look for moments and places where you can show them you are seriously trying to understand their thinking. Make your comments as a member of the audience, suggesting where more detail could be helpful to support understanding and commenting on interesting approaches. Raise questions that might push for generalization. As you move around look for big ideas and strategies from the landscape. This is a nice time to also plan which pieces of work you will select for the congress.

Facilitating the Math Congress

Review the posters and choose a few that you can use for a discussion that will deepen understanding and support growth along the landscape of learning described in the overview. There is not necessarily one best plan for a congress. There are many different plans that might all be supportive of development.

You'll want to make this congress supportive of the use of the ratio table as a tool: jumping around on it in clever ways for converting and using equivalent rates. But remember to work developmentally. If you start with an approach that shows a strong understanding of scaling for example, but one that will be difficult for most of your students to understand, you will lose many during the discussion. Think about how to scaffold your congress so that entry levels exist for those who aren't thinking multiplicatively yet. Think about how you might connect the posters you use so that the discussion that occurs actually promotes new insights.

Inside One Classroom: A Portion of the Congress

Catherine (the teacher) brings up the group she spoke with on Day Five who had to go back and re-calculate with a consistent scale factor.

Catherine: Josie, Josh, and Sasha I've got a picture of your work up on the projector here. You had to work really hard on the Very Big Batch didn't you? Please come up and tell us how you figured out what to do.

Sasha: Well at first we just knew that the numbers had to be very big, so we used big ones. But then we realized that our batch might end up too milky or too dry if we weren't careful.

Author's notes

Catherine starts with a group who has made significant

Josie: 4 liters was the clue. You told us that the milk had to be 4 liters, because Muffles had already written that in.

Josh: At first we didn't know how to get there from deciliters, but then we realized 20 deciliters was the same as 2 liters and then it was easy. We doubled the 2 liters.

Catherine: So you noticed that you were going to have to convert from deciliters to liters to compare the Very Big Batch with the others?

Josh: Yeah. Deciliters are smaller, so it takes 10 of them to make a liter and 20 are 2 liters.

Sasha: We got a little more stuck on the dekagrams, though. We were at 280 dekagrams for the Big Batch because it was times 10. And then we doubled and got 560 dekagrams for the last one.

Josie: But 560 dekagrams wouldn't be very easy to measure out! And we tried making it into grams, but that just made it worse. 5,600 grams!

Catherine: You know, it's interesting that you say that. Because I also saw another group that spent a lot of time trying to make the dekagrams simpler. Talia and Aidan, can you come up and explain what you did?

Talia: We thought the same thing as Sasha, 560 dekagrams was a weird number. Dekagrams are 10 times bigger than a gram and we looked at the chart and saw that the next step would be hectograms. They're 100 times bigger.

Aidan: Basically, hectograms are the next step. They're 10 times bigger than dekagrams, so we divided the number by 10 and got 56 hectograms.

Talia: You could even keep going and get 5.6 kilograms.

Catherine: Whoa! That's a lot of ways to measure. Let me get those on the board. Josie said is was 5,600 grams, you both got 560 dekagrams, and then you're saying that's also 56 hectograms and 5.6 kilograms? *(Catherine writes "5,600 grams = 560 dekagrams = 56 hectograms = 5.6 kilograms" as she speaks.)* Everyone turn and talk with your shoulder partner about this. *(After allowing students some time to discuss)* Pauline, I notice you and your partner got really excited about something. Could you share what you were talking about?

Pauline: We know 5,600 grams is 5.6 kilograms because 5,000 grams are 5 kilograms. So the rest of them must be right too, because you lose a zero every step.

---

progress during this investigation, knowing that their evolution of thinking will help other students find similar insights.

The students recognize that converting to larger units can make their numbers simpler, but are unsure how to convert from dekagrams since all the relationships in Appendix F are listed based on grams. During conferrals, Catherine noticed that Talia and Aidan had a strong approach to the conversion ratios and she brings them into the conversation now.

Aidan and Talia are presenting a scaling strategy rooted firmly in place value patterns and the ratios inherent in the metric system. Catherine makes sure students have a chance to discuss and puzzle about these patterns.

Josh: I see it. Like from deciliters to liters we lost the zero in the 20 because it took 10 deciliters to make one liter. And it was 10 grams in a dekagram, then 10 dekagrams in a hectogram? Wait... I thought hectograms were 100.

Aidan: They are, but it's 100 grams and 10 dekagrams because each one is 10 grams. *(Aidan sees looks of confusion from Josh and some other peers, but doesn't know how to explain further.)*

Catherine: Aidan, what you're saying sounds kind of like money to me. A dollar is 100 cents, but it's also 10 dimes, right?

Aidan: Exactly! A dime is 10 pennies and a dollar is 100 pennies, so that means it must be 10 dimes, too. Because 100 is 10 x 10.

Josie: That's where the 10 is! 100 is 10x10 and 1,000 is 10x10x10. Each step up is one zero bigger than the last one because it's another 10 times bigger or smaller.

Money is a powerful model for decimals and place value patterns, and so Catherine invokes it to help Aidan express his argument in a way that is more accessible to many of his peers.

Minilesson: A String of Related Problems

This string is designed to help students continue to use multiplicative structuring, more flexibly converting one unit to another using strategies based on ratio thinking. Doing it after the congress instead of at the beginning of math workshop is beneficial today because the congress supported the ability to scale and this gives students a chance to practice what they were discussing.

Represent the problems on a t-chart like the one below, one problem at a time, moving from the top to the bottom of the chart, and invite students to share their conversion strategies. As they do, record their thinking on the t-chart.

The String:

Milliliters	Centiliters	Deciliters	Liters
			4
	800		
	200		
6000			
3000			
		100	
9000			
			12

Reflections on the Day

Math workshop began today with a preparation for a gallery walk. As you moved around and conferred you may have noticed that more and more students are now starting to use ratio thinking. A congress provided students an opportunity to share strategies for scaling and explore the big idea that equivalent measurements can be exchanged. The minilesson was designed to encourage the use of ratio thinking, specifically the use of multiplication and division by 10, 100 and 1,000. Each day you should see your children making progress on the landscape. Remember to document growth on the landscape in the overview. As this week continues, more ratio tables will be used for conversions, so keep the copies of Appendices F and G showing the equivalencies available.

DAY SEVEN

CHOCOLATE NUT TRUFFLES

Materials Needed

The Grams and Liters Charts (Appendices F and G, extra copies for student reference)

Muffles' Recipe Chart for Chocolate Nut Truffles (Appendix H, one per pair of students)

Pencils

Drawing paper or several sheets of copy paper

Blank Chart Paper for posters (sticky note style is best as it makes taping on the walls unnecessary)

Markers

Today begins with another minilesson designed to support multiplicative structuring and the flexible conversion of standard units of liquid volume. Then students work on another of Muffles' recipes: chocolate nut truffles. Once again students work on converting centiliters, deciliters, and liters and kilograms, dekagrams, and grams. This context also uses a ratio table as a tool, and as students work to generate recipes for larger batches, many opportunities will occur once again for rich discussions on equivalence and proportional reasoning related to measurement.

Day Seven Outline

Minilesson: A String of Related Problems
❖ Work on a string of related liquid volume problems designed to encourage students to convert fluently using multiplicative structuring.

Developing the Context
❖ Tell the story of Pierre wanting charts for his favorite type of Muffles' truffles, chocolate nut, using Appendix H.
❖ Remind students of the equivalence of the units shown on Appendices F and G and ensure that they have copies handy.
❖ Ask students to work in pairs on Appendix H, making a recipe chart for various batches of Muffles' chocolate nut truffles.

Supporting the Investigation
❖ Confer with children as they work, noting the strategies they use and how they convert.
❖ As students finish, ask them to prepare a poster to convince others of their solutions and important things they have noticed along the way as they worked. These posters will be used on Day Eight in a gallery walk and congress.

Minilesson: A String of Related Problems

This string is designed in a similar fashion to the others you have been using throughout this unit. Its purpose, as with the others, is to keep familiarizing students with conversions. It also helps to deepen students' understanding of place value. Represent the problems on a t-chart like the one below, showing only one problem at a time, moving from the top to the bottom of the chart, and invite students to share their conversion strategies. As they do, record their thinking on the t-chart.

Milliliters	Liters	Kiloliters
		1
		2
		4
		8
		16
		10
		5
		6

Inside One Classroom: A Portion of the Minilesson

Catherine (the teacher): 1 kiloliter. How many liters would that be?

Josie: 1,000?

Catherine: Tell us more about your thinking. Why do you think it is 1,000?

Josie: It's 10 times to get to hectoliters, then 10 times to get to dekaliters, and 10 times again to get to liters.

Catherine: How many of you agree? *(Everyone's hands go up so Catherine writes "1,000" in the liters column.)* You said a very interesting thing, Josie. You said, "I multiplied by 10, three times." So you're saying that 1,000 is 10x10x10? Everyone turn and talk to a shoulder partner about this. *(After a few minutes, Catherine resumes whole group discussion.)* So you turned and talked. Did anyone have an interesting partner? *(The children are rather surprised by her question as most were ready to share their own thinking. No one puts their hands up.)*

Catherine: Well that's a pity. Not one interesting partner in our whole math community? Turn and talk again then! Be an interesting partner. *(After a few minutes...)* Sasha, You had an interesting partner?

Author's notes

Catherine starts the minilesson by writing the first problem in the appropriate column. She asks about the liters first to encourage the children to see that 1,000 liters equals 1 kiloliter. She provided pair talk to give her students time to reflect on the relationships.

By asking who had an interesting partner, Catherine implicitly communicates that when you turn and talk you

MUFFLES' MEASUREMENT MODELS PART TWO: THE METRIC SYSTEM

Sasha: Yes, My partner was Juan. He said he thinks the number of zeroes tells you how many times you multiplied by ten.

Catherine: Wow! I can see why you thought he was interesting! What did you think about his idea?

Sasha: It must be. 100 is 10x10 and that has 2 zeroes. When I did 1,000 x 1,000 to get the milliliters, I got 1,000,000. I was thinking maybe you could just add the zeroes up. 1,000 x 1,000...each 1,000 has 3 zeroes, so 3 + 3 = 6, and that is what I got a 1 with 6 zeroes.

Catherine: This is so interesting. Mathematicians actually have a way of representing how many times ten has been multiplied by itself. 10x10 like Sasha said is 100. And so it can be written as 10^2, and 1,000 like Josie said is 10x10x10, so that would be 10^3. And then 1,000 x 1,000 is 10^6. When numbers are written small and up above another number like these, they represent how many times you multiplied the numbered by itself and they are called exponents. So what I'm wondering is if we were multiplying $10^2 \times 10^3$, could we just add the exponents and that is how many zeroes there would be in the answer? Turn and talk about this. Juan I'm wondering if this is connected to your idea.

should be an interesting partner. The talk should be "accountable talk."

Note how Catherine does not ask Juan to explain. Since it is his idea he won't have any trouble explaining. Asking Sasha to explain his idea and to decide what she thinks of it pushes her to think harder about what Juan said. Catherine will bring him back in after to see if Sasha understood his idea and if he wants to add anything. But first, the conversation continues focused now on powers of 10, and this provides Catherine an opportunity to introduce exponents.

Developing the Context

Use Appendices F, G, and H as you tell the following story. Remember to make the context come alive!

Pierre is very pleased with the work Patricio is doing to help his shop be ready for opening day. He knows Muffles' most popular truffle is dark chocolate and he assumes it will be the most popular flavor in his shop as well. His own personal favorite, however, is chocolate nut and he asks Patricio to make a chart for that flavor, too, just in case a lot of customers are like him and find that flavor delectable.

Pierre starts the chart using the Basic Recipe that Muffles provided, but Patricio offers to finish it for him. But then Patricio notices that the chart is different. There are no headings on this chart, except The Basic Recipe and The Big Batch. And there is no Very Big Batch even on the chart! "Uh-oh...," thinks Patricio. "I'm in trouble... I've got another problem to crack. How do I know if Pierre was going to triple, or quadruple? Maybe he wasn't..."

Remind children that the basic recipe is in kilograms and liters. Make sure they understand that this chart may have some aspects similar to the other, but it may also be different. Suggest they look very carefully at the clues Pierre left for Patricio and remind them of the equivalent units listed on Appendices F and G. Assign math partners and send students off to investigate what Patricio should write on this new chart.

Behind the Numbers

This investigation is much more difficult than the one introduced on Day Five as the headings are missing. It is not possible to tell how much to scale the basic recipe up by using the heading as the scale factor. The only way students can determine the scaling factor is to determine the ratio of the number of truffles each batch makes. If the Basic Recipe makes 200 truffles, then to make 20 truffles the recipe only needs 1/10 as much milk chocolate, cream, and nuts. By now students should be more comfortable using place value patterns to scale within the metric system. Encourage them to jump around and do what they know first. For example, if they realize that the Big Batch is ten times larger than the Basic Recipe, they will likely recognize that they need to multiply each of the ingredients by 10 as well. Scaling with division is trickier, but students may think of 1 kilogram as 1,000 grams, scaling down to 100 grams for the 20-truffle batch. Alternately, they might even use 1/10 or 0.1 kg. Samples of children's work from field testing are provided in *Supporting the Investigation* to help you anticipate what your children might do.

Supporting the Investigation

As you move around conferring, take note of how children are moving on the table. Look for children who just assume this chart will be the same ratios as the chart they made on Day Five and Six. Do they just write Doubling, Tripling, and Quadrupling across the top without looking at the numbers given in the columns? As you confer with students who do this, query them afterward about whether the headings work.

On the other hand you may see lots of your children at this point able to use the place value patterns and this may be a place to celebrate with them what they have learned. A sample of children's work is provided on the next two pages. Notice that, while making strong use of multiplication and division by 10 and 100, the students have mistakenly listed "100 mililiters or 1 centiliter" in one column and in the next, "1 centiliter [or] 10 liters" (they probably mean mililiters rather than liters). These students realize that a bigger unit will have a smaller number value, but do not consistently base their conversion on the relative size of the two units. While the arithmetic is not difficult, keeping track of zeros and the relationship between units is crucial in the metric system. This is another reason it is so valuable for students to articulate their thinking on posters, examine each others' work carefully, and discuss their ideas in math congresses and minilessons!

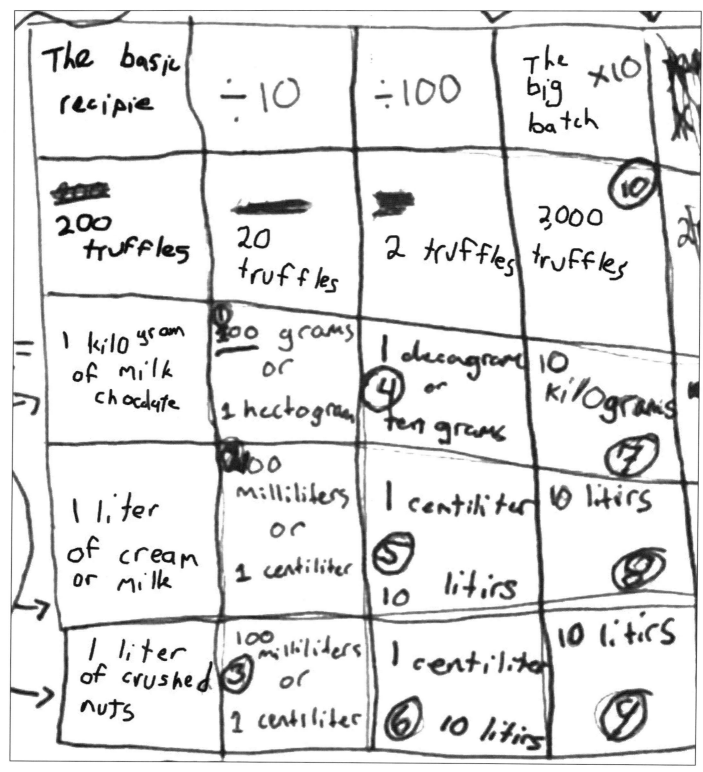

Figure 3. A close-up of the student chart on the following page.

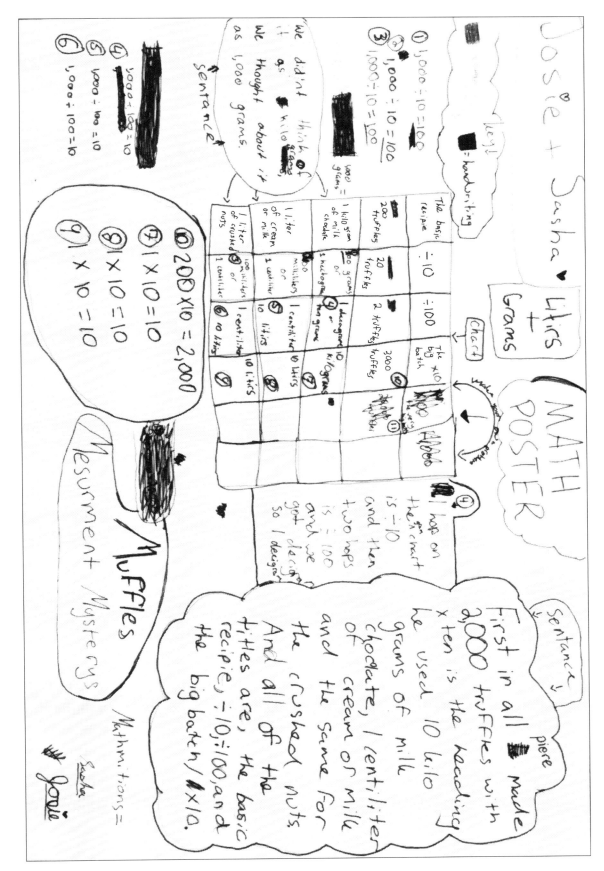

Figure 4. The full student poster

Reflections on the Day

Today you likely saw a lot of progress even though this investigation was difficult. Without the headings given, children really had to examine the proportionality of the ingredients. Although they may have had to think hard about this, the difficulty level most likely challenged them in a beneficial way to examine relationships. Tomorrow the relationships noticed will become the focus of discussion in a gallery walk and the congress.

DAY EIGHT

THE CHART FOR THE TRUFFLES

Materials Needed

Students' work from Day Seven

Markers and Pencils

Sticky notes (about 3 per student)

Today begins with a minilesson on converting grams to kilograms. Students then add finishing touches to their posters from Day Seven and a gallery walk ensues. After the gallery walk a congress is held to discuss more deeply a few of the pieces.

Day Eight Outline

Minilesson: A String of Related Problems
❖ Work on a string of related problems designed to encourage students to convert grams to kilograms.
❖ Introduce number pairs as another way to represent the data.

Facilitating the Gallery Walk
❖ Confer with children as they put finishing touches to their posters, asking them to consider the most important things they want to tell their audience about smart ways to convert.
❖ Conduct a gallery walk to allow students time to reflect and comment on each other's posters on the investigation started on Day Seven.

Facilitating the Math Congress
❖ Convene students at the meeting area to discuss a few important ideas about converting efficiently from one unit of measure to another.

Minilesson: A String of Related Problems

This string is designed in a similar fashion to the others you have been using throughout this unit. Its purpose, as with the others, is to keep familiarizing students with conversions. Today the focus is grams and kilograms. Represent the problems on a t-chart like the one below, showing only one problem at a time, moving from the top to the bottom of the chart, and invite students to share their conversion strategies. As they do, record their thinking on the t-chart.

The string:

grams	kilograms
16,000	
8,000	
4,000	
12,000	
32,000	
24,000	
	48
	160

Since this ratio table has only two columns, as children produce the kilograms for each of the problems, this is a nice time to introduce number pairs as another way of modeling the data: (16000, 16), (8000, 8), (4000, 4), etc. You can just explain that mathematicians sometimes represent the numbers on a ratio table that way. They think about it as input/output (or x and y coordinates) and they pair the input with the output.

Facilitating the Gallery Walk

Ask students to return to the posters they began on Day Seven, adding any finishing touches they desire. As they work, move around and confer, asking them to consider the most important things they want to tell their audience about smart ways to convert. Remind them that it is not necessary to write about everything they did, but instead to concentrate on convincing their audience about the important things they discovered and want to defend.

Facilitating the Math Congress

Review the posters and choose a few that you can use for a discussion that will deepen understanding and support growth along the landscape of learning described in the overview. There is not necessarily one best plan for a congress. There are many different plans that might all be supportive of development.

You'll want to make this congress supportive of the use of place value and multiplication and division by ten. Some big ideas about multiplication, equivalent rates, and proportional reasoning, and targeted strategies, such as scaling and using partial products with the ratio table as a tool for thinking, are important things to notice. Remember to work developmentally and think about how to scaffold your congress. Think about how you might use the congress so that the discussion that occurs actually promotes new insights.

Reflections on the Day

Math workshop began today with a minilesson on converting grams to kilograms. Students were introduced to number pairs as another way to model the data on the charts. In the gallery walk and subsequent congress you may have noticed that more and more students are now using proportional reasoning. Are they able to go across a row using multiplication and division by ten where appropriate? Are they also scaling by one thousand or other powers of ten? Each day you should see your children making progress on the landscape. Remember to document the growth on the landscape—the learning pathway of each child.

DAY NINE

PRICES BY WEIGHT

Materials Needed

The Price Chart, (Appendix I, one per pair of students)

Pencils

Drawing paper or several sheets of copy paper

Blank Chart Paper for posters (sticky note style is best as it makes taping on the walls unnecessary)

Markers

Today begins with another minilesson on converting grams to kilograms. Following the minilesson a new context is developed. Pierre wants to sell his truffles by weight like Muffles and he asks Patricio to help with one more task before he leaves. He weighs his dark chocolate truffles and he finds that 50 of his truffles weigh ½ a kilogram, or 500 grams. What does each truffle weigh and how much should he charge?

Day Nine Outline

Minilesson: A String of Related Problems
- Work on a string of related problems designed to encourage students to convert grams to kilograms fluently using the ratio table as a tool for thinking.

Developing the Context
- Use Appendix I and tell the story of Muffles' Price Chart.
- Send students off in pairs to work on the chart.

Supporting the Investigation
- Move around the room supporting and challenging where needed.
- Celebrate the strategies you see and then convene students at the meeting area to discuss a few important ideas about converting efficiently from one unit of measure to another.
- Ensure that a final group consensus exists for the numbers on the chart as it will be needed on Day Ten.

MUFFLES' MEASUREMENT MODELS PART TWO: THE METRIC SYSTEM

Minilesson: A String of Related Problems

This string is designed in a similar fashion to the others you have been using throughout this unit. Its purpose, as with the others, is to keep familiarizing students with conversions. It also helps students use multiplicative structuring to convert more flexibly from one unit to another, using strategies based on proportional reasoning. Represent the problems on a ratio table like the one below, showing only one problem at a time, moving from the top to the bottom of the model, and invite students to share their conversion strategies. As they do, record their thinking on the t-chart.

The String:

Cupcakes	grams	kilograms
10	500	
20		
5		
15		
30		
35		

Developing the Context

Use Appendix I as you tell the following story. If you have a smart board, you can display the image. Remember to make the context come alive!

> *Pierre is very pleased with all the work Patricio has done to help his franchise of Muffles' Truffles be successful. He has recipe charts for some of his favorite truffles; he has signs posted 500 meters away to entice people to come, and he even has signs out telling his customers how long the wait will be to get to the counter.*
>
> *There is just one more thing to do. He needs a price chart. Pierre makes four columns: one for the number of truffles, one for the weight in grams, one for the weight in kilograms, and one for the cost.*
>
> *Pierre begins filling in his new chart. He writes in the first row: 50 truffles, 500 grams. "I will charge $2.50 per 50 grams for my truffles," Pierre thinks to himself, and so he writes that on the new price chart, too, in the row where it says 50 grams. But just as he was about to continue, the delivery truck bringing chocolate came. "Patricio will need to finish this," he thought to himself. "Patricio... where are you? I need some help! I have another job for you..."*

Assign math partners and send students off to investigate what Patricio should write on this new chart.

Supporting the Investigation

As you move around conferring, take note of how children are moving on the ratio table from the minilesson. Today is a good day to celebrate as you move around: celebrate how easily they are moving around the chart. The decimals, however, might be a big challenge for some. As they work remind them of conversations they have had over the week about how multiplication and division by ten just moves the number to the left or to the right. Thinking of 0.5 kilograms as ½, or as 50 cents, or half a dollar might be helpful. Fifty cents divided by ten produces a nickel (0.05), and this divided by 5 produces a penny (0.01). The congress should center on the kilogram column. At this point in the unit children most likely have enough of an understanding of place value that introducing them to decimals in the context with the ratio table as a tool, with landmark decimals, will be enough support to engender meaning.

Reflections on the Day

Math workshop began today with a minilesson on converting grams to kilograms. Children then continued to work with these conversions as they developed a price chart for Pierre. Throughout this unit children have been supported to develop the use of the ratio table as a powerful model and tool for conversions of units of measure, but also for multiplication. Today is a day to celebrate with them on the variety of strategies they have developed. Tomorrow their learning can be extended as they develop their own pricing charts and choose their own numbers.

DAY TEN

CHOOSE YOUR OWN NUMBERS

Materials Needed

Pencils

Drawing paper or several sheets of copy paper

Blank Chart Paper for posters (sticky note style is best as it makes taping on the walls unnecessary)

Markers

Today begins with another minilesson on converting grams to kilograms. Following the minilesson children are invited to add numbers of their own choosing to the price chart. Today is a chance to get further evidence on each child's facility with measurement conversions and their ability to use the ratio table as a tool for thinking. Let them inquire and challenge themselves. Big numbers, fractions, decimals, anything goes! But encourage them to pick numbers where they can use relationships and numbers they can have fun solving!

Day Ten Outline

Minilesson: A String of Related Problem
❖ Work on a string of related problems designed to encourage students to convert grams to kilograms fluently using the ratio table as a tool for thinking.

Developing the Context
❖ Explain how proud you are of the many strategies everyone has developed over the last two weeks. Point out how powerful the ratio table is as a model for measurement conversions.
❖ Suggest they use all of the strategies they have developed to add more numbers to the price chart.

Supporting the Investigation
❖ Move around and confer, remembering to clarify what you see, celebrate the strategies you see children trying, and support and challenge as needed.

Minilesson: A String of Related Problems

This string is designed in a similar fashion to the others you have been using throughout this unit. Its purpose, as with the others, is to keep familiarizing students with conversions. Represent the problems on a ratio table like the one below, showing only one problem at a time, moving from the top to the bottom of the chart, and invite students to share their conversion strategies. These numbers will remind them of the chart they did on Day Nine so make sure those papers are not available. Using the same numbers is purposeful to ensure everyone is comfortable when they go off to work on the subsequent investigation. Leave the results of the minilesson, the finished chart, up on the board so that children can make use of it as they work.

Grams	Kilograms	Cost
500	0.5	$25
1000		
2000	2	
200		
100		
50		

Developing the Context

Explain that since this is the last day of the unit, you think it might be fun for everyone to add other numbers of their choosing to Muffles' price chart. Provide them with drawing paper so that they can make their own ratio table, but provide as a constraint that they have to use Muffles' rate: 50 grams cost $2.50. Tell them they can pick the numbers and should challenge themselves, but remind them to make use of relationships and to use the variety of strategies they have developed. Point out that the chart from the minilesson is still up and they have their work from Day Nine, then assign math partners and send students off to choose their own numbers.

Supporting the Investigation

As you move around conferring, take note of how children are moving on the ratio table. Note how they challenge themselves. Do they use partial products to find numbers other than the ones on the chart? Do they use generalized scaling? Are the decimals as they convert to kilograms too difficult or are they making use of multiplication and division by ten and producing decimals with meaning based on place value? The money model might be helping them. If you like you can challenge students to add more columns and convert the cost in dollars to all quarters, or all dimes.

Reflections on the Unit

The mathematician Samuel Karlin once said, "The purpose of models is not to fit the data but to sharpen the questions." In this, the second of two measurement units, the ratio table and the double number line were developed and used to sharpen students' questions. Students constructed proportional reasoning; they used partial products and scaling. With these models, equivalence and measurement conversions took on new meanings.

The models were developed through a number of different investigations. Students explored the length of the line of customers and placed signs along the way in ten minute intervals to show the rate of time to length and the number of customers. In Part One they formulated various strategies for making equivalent measurements using Customary U.S. units for length, then later for liquid volume and weight as they scaled up Muffles' recipes to make larger batches. They even examined ratios with fractional amounts. In Part Two they worked with the metric system, deepened their understanding of place value, and began to work with decimals making use of the money model.

Often mathematics has been taught in our schools as if it were a dead language. It was something that mathematicians had created in the past—something that needed to be learned, practiced, and applied. When the definition of mathematics shifts toward the activity of mathematizing one's own lived world, the constructive nature of the discipline and its connection to problem solving become clear.

Appendix A1: Muffles' Truffles Shop

Appendix A2: Which tool?

"Which tool should I use?" asks Patricio.

Appendix B: Patricio's Line

Patricio uses the trundle wheel to mark 100 meters. He does this five times. Now how long is the line?

How many meters?

How many kilometers?

How many dekameters?

How many hectometers?

How many decimeters?

How many centimeters?

Appendix C: The Meters Chart

kilometer	1,000 times bigger than a meter
hectometer	100 times bigger than a meter
dekameter	10 times bigger than a meter
meter	
decimeter	10 times smaller than a meter
centimeter	100 times smaller than a meter
millimeter	1,000 times smaller than a meter

Appendix D: Patricio's Model (1 of 2)

The next morning Pierre showed Patricio his signs. He had written, "½ kilometer to Muffles' Truffles" on one sign, and then 400 meters, 300 meters, 200 meters, and 100 meters on the others.

Now Patricio had another problem. If he put the time on those signs, the time would be so long no one would wait in line! Patricio decided to use Pierre's signs, but as ads. "People will be curious when they see these signs," he thinks to himself, "and they'll come to the shop. Pierre's signs will help. But now how do I figure out where to put the wait signs with the time on them, so customers will know how long they will have to wait to get to the counter?"

Patricio had an idea. He thought, "Whenever I feel stuck with a math problem, I know that if I try to model it somehow I have a way to start." So he built a model like the one he had made for Muffles, except he did it in meters. 3 meters for every 6 customers, and that would take 10 minutes.

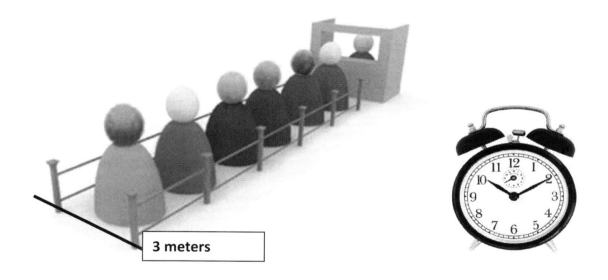

Appendix D: Patricio's Model (2 of 2)

Next Patricio drew a long line to represent the line of customers and he began marking where the signs for every 10 minutes should go.

10 minutes

3 meters

6 people

Help Patricio finish modeling the problem. How long is this new line of customers and how long will it take for the last customer in line to get to the counter? (Remember, there are 60 minutes in an hour and 60 seconds in a minute.)

Meters	Dekameters	Minutes	Seconds	Hours	People
3		10			6

Is Patricio's model a helpful tool for solving the problem?

How did you use it?

Appendix E: Muffles' Recipe Chart for Dark Chocolate Truffles

The Basic Recipe	Doubling	Tripling	Quadrupling	The Big Batch	The VERY Big Batch
Makes 60 truffles	Makes 120 truffles			Makes 600 truffles	
28 dekagrams of dark chocolate					
2 deciliters of milk					4 liters of milk

Appendix F: The Grams Chart

kilogram	1,000 times bigger than a gram
hectogram	100 times bigger than a gram
dekagram	10 times bigger than a gram
gram	
decigram	10 times smaller than a gram
centigram	100 times smaller than a gram
milligram	1,000 times smaller than a gram

Appendix G: The Liters Chart

kiloliter	1,000 times bigger than a liter
hectoliter	100 times bigger than a liter
dekaliter	10 times bigger than a liter
liter	
deciliter	10 times smaller than a liter
centiliter	100 times smaller than a liter
milliliter	1,000 times smaller than a liter

Appendix H: Muffles' Recipe Chart for Chocolate Nut Truffles

The Basic Recipe			The Big Batch
Makes 200 truffles	Makes 20 truffles	Makes 2 truffles	Makes 2,000 truffles
1 kilogram of milk chocolate			
1 liter of cream or milk			
1 liter of crushed nuts			

MUFFLES' MEASUREMENT MODELS PART TWO: THE METRIC SYSTEM

Appendix I: The Price Chart

The Price Chart

Truffles	Grams	Kilograms	Price
50	500		
	50		$2.50
	10		
	1,000		
	250		

Made in the USA
Columbia, SC
07 January 2019